REVOLUTIONARY FRIENDS

General George Washington *and the* Marquis de Lafayette

Selene Castrovilla

ILLUSTRATED BY Drazen Kozjan

CALKINS CREEK
AN IMPRINT OF
BOYDS MILLS & KANE
New York

Page 40: Collection of the U.S. House of Representatives.
Images courtesy of the Architect of the Capitol.

Calkins Creek
An imprint of Boyds Mills & Kane, a division of Astra Publishing House
calkinscreekbooks.com
Printed in the United States of America

ISBN: 978-1-59078-880-6 (hc)
ISBN: 978-1-63592-508-1 (eBook)

Library of Congress Control Number: 2012949044

First edition

10 9 8 7 6 5

Designed by Barbara Grzeslo
The text is set in Aldus and Bell Martellus.
The illustrations are done in pen and ink and digital color.

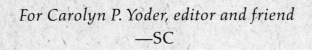

For Carolyn P. Yoder, editor and friend
—SC

For Jason S., Rob B., Pat H., Steve B., and Eric O.
—DK

Thanks to David A. Clary, Alan Hoffman, Benoit Guizard, Almut Spaulding,
and all the American Friends of Lafayette; Mary V. Thompson, research historian,
George Washington's Mount Vernon Estate, Museum, and Gardens;
my intrepid Revolutionary War expert, Andrew Batten; my research assistant,
Pascale Laforest; my French expert, Mikki Kirdahy; and, of course, my sons—
best in the world!
—SC

I would like to thank Mary V. Thompson, research historian,
George Washington's Mount Vernon Estate, Museum, and Gardens
(mountvernon.org); David A. Clary with the American Friends of Lafayette;
and Andrew Batten, former executive director, Fraunces Tavern Museum,
New York, New York, for their careful review of the artwork.
Also, I would like to acknowledge the references I used for my illustrations:
George Washington: American Symbol, edited by Barbara J. Mitnick;
For Liberty and Glory: Washington, Lafayette, and Their Revolutions by James R.
Gaines; and *An Illustrated Encyclopedia of Uniforms from 1775–1778:
The American Revolutionary War* by Digby Smith and Kevin F. Kiley.
And thanks to editor Carolyn P. Yoder and art director Barbara Grzeslo
of Calkins Creek.
—DK

July 31, 1777

C'est le moment!
Lafayette quivered with excitement. What a
thrill to dine at City Tavern, among American patriots
he so admired.

Was he dreaming?

Mais non.

Dreams did not offer the succulent aromas of
fine dining or the sharp scent of dark ale.

This was real.

Magnifique!

*Having to
choose between the
slavery that everyone believes
he has the right to impose upon
me, and liberty, which called me
to glory, I departed.*
—MARQUIS DE LAFAYETTE,
EXPLAINING WHY HE LEFT FRANCE
FOR AMERICA

Nineteen-year-old Marie-Joseph-Paul-Yves-Roch-Gilbert du Motier, Marquis de Lafayette, ventured a great deal to get there.

He had always felt a call to glory.

His heart enlisted when he learned of the Americans' struggle. The rest of his body proved more difficult.

The French king denied his request to leave.

Au contraire!

Lafayette paid for his own ship and slipped out of France, spending fifty-four stomach-wrenching days at sea.

Then he had suffered a month of broken carriages, lame horses, and nightly mosquito raids as he trekked hundreds of miles.

Never before had such a glorious cause attracted the attention of mankind; it was the final struggle of liberty, and its defeat would have left it neither asylum nor hope. . . . When I first heard of [the American Revolution], my heart was enlisted, and I thought only of joining the colors.

—Marquis de Lafayette

Here he was, finally.

And in the same room as the great George Washington.

Très bien!

City Tavern was jammed, and humming with animated voices and a steady clinking of glasses. Lafayette spotted the forty-five-year-old commander in chief immediately. Washington's figure and manner separated him from the surrounding crowd.

Lafayette had to meet him.

Maintenant!

General Washington came to Philadelphia, and M. de Lafayette beheld for the first time that great man. Although he was surrounded by officers and citizens, it was impossible to mistake for a moment his majestic figure and deportment; nor was he less distinguished by the noble affability of his manner.

—MARQUIS DE LAFAYETTE, ON HIS FIRST MEETING WITH WASHINGTON

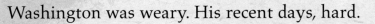

Washington was weary. His recent days, hard.

The British lay near.

Were they readying to strike?

Washington's ragtag troops could not match the hearty redcoats.

Members of Congress badgered Washington. Why wasn't he preparing Philadelphia for attack?

Peck, peck, peck! Their voices pricked his brain. Washington was tired of sharing strategies with men deaf to reason.

The moment, although important to the common cause, was peculiarly unfavourable to strangers. The Americans were displeased with the pretensions, and disgusted with the conduct, of many Frenchmen.
—MARQUIS DE LAFAYETTE, ON THE ATMOSPHERE WHEN HE ARRIVED IN PHILADELPHIA

Now there was someone else to consider—tonight's guest, the young Frenchman who gawked in admiration.

There was an important reason to treat Lafayette cordially. Of noble birth, he could improve relations with France—an ally America needed.

This explained why Congress had given Lafayette an honorary position in the army. No salary and no command—only a major general's sash.

Washington was prepared to discount Lafayette. The previous French recruits had been snobbish, bossy, and unwilling to learn English. On top of it all, Lafayette was scrawny and young—and inexperienced.

What possible good could he be?

Still, it was in America's best interest to invite Lafayette into Washington's military family.

Lafayette was blissfully unaware of Washington's opinions.

He had adopted the motto *cur non*—"why not." Having come this far, why not go further?

Lafayette was anxious to be trained and eager to communicate. He had studied English while on the rough sea.

He adored America. And because Washington represented America, Lafayette idolized him.

Washington approached.

Enchanté!

The commander complimented Lafayette on his noble spirit and the sacrifices he had made. He invited Lafayette to live in his quarters.

Voilà!

To Lafayette, the cementing of their bond was as simple as that.

I have a friend. . . . That friend is General Washington. This excellent man, whose talents and virtues I admired, and whom I have learnt to revere as I know him better, has now become my intimate friend: his affectionate interest in me instantly won my heart. I am established in his house, and we live together like two attached brothers, with mutual confidence and cordiality. This friendship renders me as happy as I can possibly be in this country.
—Marquis de Lafayette, in a letter to his wife

Lafayette charmed everyone at headquarters.
Did that include Washington?
Perhaps . . .
But Washington had other matters on his mind.
His army was in poor shape, indeed.
Just days after they met, he invited Lafayette
to review the troops.

An embarrassment! Eleven thousand ill-armed,
barely clothed men who did not look ready to fight.

"We must feel embarrassed," said General Washington, . . . "to exhibit ourselves before an officer who has just quitted French troops." "It is to learn, and not to teach, that I come hither," replied M. de Lafayette; and that modest tone, which was not common in Europeans, produced a very good effect.
—MARQUIS DE LAFAYETTE, DESCRIBING THE INSPECTION OF THE TROOPS

The British, however, *were* ready—and close.
Two hundred English warships had landed only a few miles away.
Une situation grave.
Lafayette saw the fear in Philadelphians' faces.
He observed Washington carefully.
What would the commander do?

Washington needed to raise spirits.
His troops would parade through the streets.
Drums and fifes in quickstep, green sprigs in hats.
In front, Washington on horseback.
And beside him, Lafayette.

A parade was **bon**, but . . .
Lafayette wanted a command.
Burning to prove himself, he nagged Washington
and Congress.
S'il vous plaît!

Washington was experiencing an emotion he didn't often feel.
He had grown fond of Lafayette.
Washington appealed to Congress. Would they give the marquis
a chance? Congress refused.

Washington sat Lafayette down. He apologized for the distress the young man felt. Although he had no power to grant a command, Washington did have affection to offer.

He told Lafayette to think of him as "friend and father."

A father!

Quel honneur.

Lafayette was touched in the deepest way.

But could he ever experience his glory?

Just after his twentieth birthday, the chance came.

On September 11, the British were coming.

Zut alors!

Advancing through Brandywine Creek, thirty miles outside Philadelphia.

Washington was determined to block them.
But where in the creek would the British cross?
There were so many fords.
Washington knew of some. . . .
Did the British know of others?
Worse, a heavy fog had set in that morning.
Spotting the enemy would prove impossible.

At headquarters near a main ford, Lafayette waited with
Washington for word.
The news: devastating.
The British had broken through several of Brandywine's fords!
The American troops were panicking!
Lafayette was on fire to join in.
He requested permission from Washington.

Washington stared at Lafayette.
The Americans were outnumbered, even with the
reinforcements he had just sent.
The marquis could get himself killed!
But he looked so excited to prove himself.
Washington told him to proceed.

Through the smoky haze and British musket blasts, Lafayette spotted terrified American soldiers fleeing.

Sacrebleu!

There was only one thing to do.

Lafayette dismounted.

He raced into the ranks—a one-man rallying tour de force.

Sparked by Lafayette's courage, the soldiers returned to the fight.

With renewed vigor, they advanced.

The noises were deafening: weapons blasting, wounded men screaming. And the scent of gunpowder, suffocating.

Mon Dieu!

A ball passed through Lafayette's left leg.

Oh! The pain!

But he waged on . . . ignoring the fiery spasms . . .

Until . . .

The enemy united all their fire upon the centre: the confusion became extreme; and it was whilst M. de Lafayette was rallying the troops that a ball passed through his leg.
—MARQUIS DE LAFAYETTE, ON THE BATTLE OF BRANDYWINE

The remaining American forces gave way and headed into the woods.

Blood spilled from his boot.

He needed help—*immédiatement!*

Gimat, his aide, appeared at his side and hastily wrapped the wound.

The enemy was near—they were closing in.

Lafayette was almost taken.

Gimat found a horse and boosted Lafayette up.

Allez!

His leg throbbing in protest, Lafayette rode twelve miles to a stone bridge—on the heels of the frenzied retreating American troops.

He stopped them and established a degree of order.

Duties done, Lafayette dropped—from pain, from exhaustion.

The Americans had lost.

But they'd fight another day.

Carried to a house nearby, Lafayette lay on a table. His wound needed dressing.

In tramped Washington and his officers—weary, ravenous.

Lafayette managed a joke, asking not to be eaten.

Washington was grave.

There were enough casualties that day.

He would not lose Lafayette. He *could* not lose him.

He instructed the doctor, "Take charge of him as if he were my son, for I love him with the same affection."

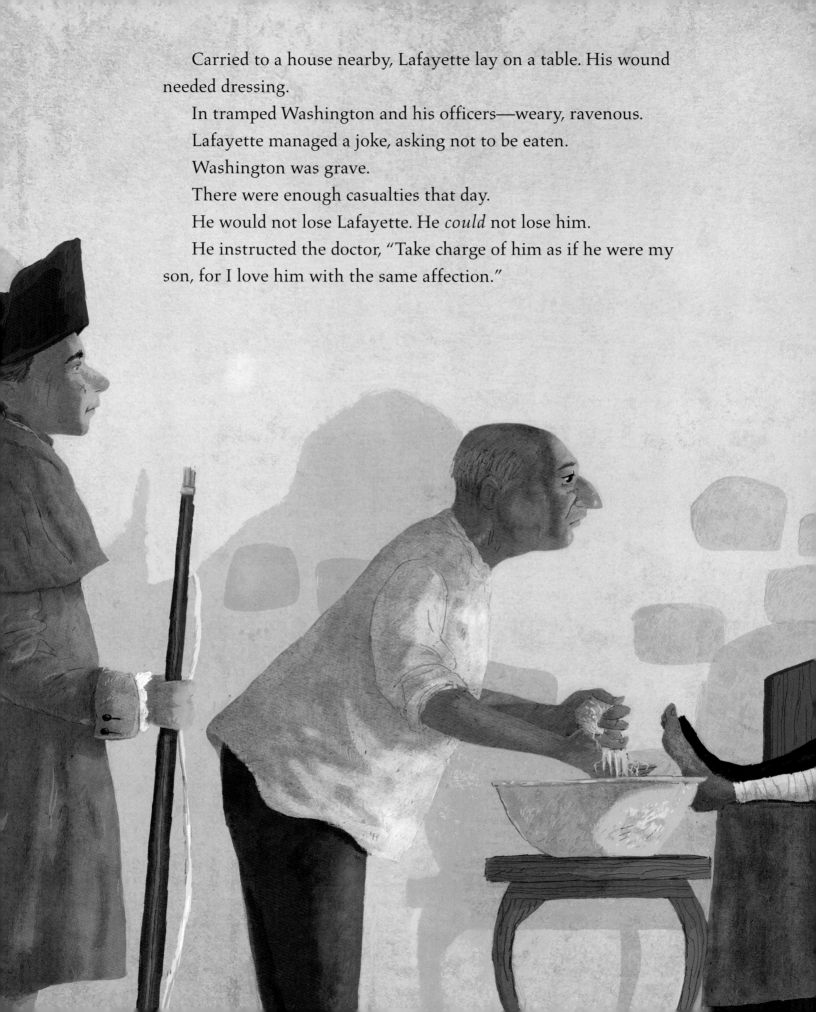

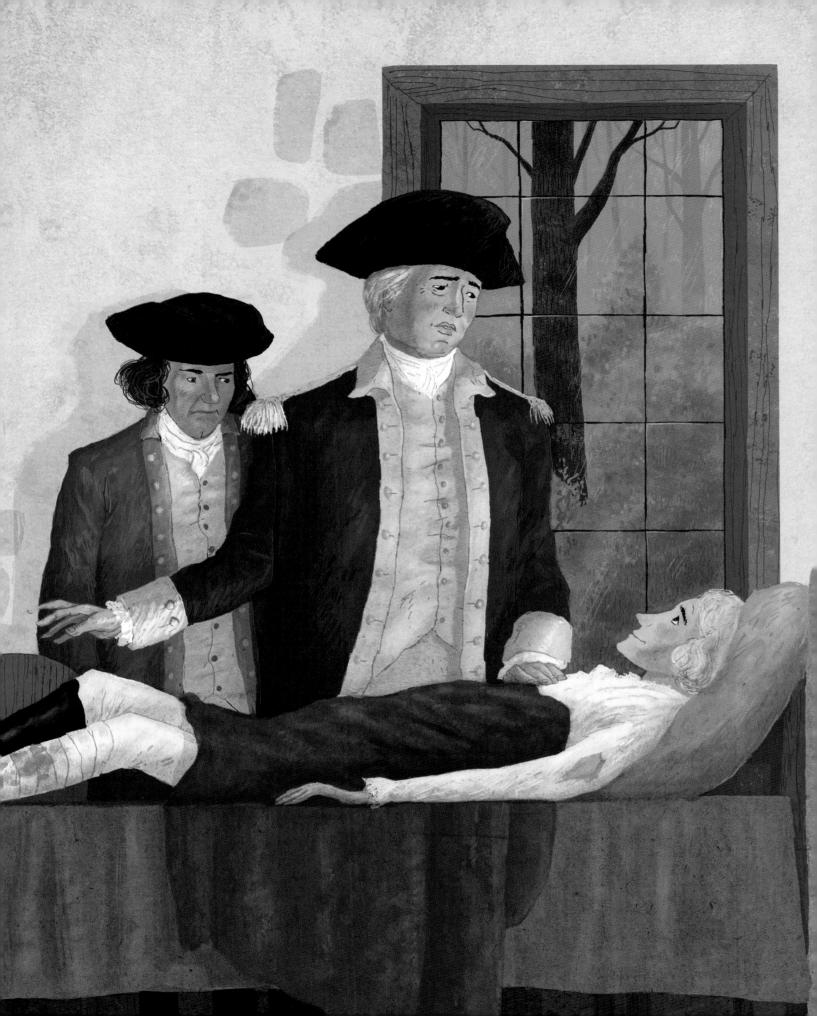

From that moment on, Washington and Lafayette's commitment was sealed; they were devoted to each other.

"General Washington's confidence in other people always had limits, but for M. de Lafayette it had no bounds, because it came from the heart," Lafayette recalled in his memoir.

In a 1777 letter, Lafayette wrote: "I admire [Washington] more each day for the beauty of his character and his spirit."

Lafayette's injury left him bedridden for just over a month. Impatient, he headed back to the ranks—and Washington—with an open wound he couldn't cover with a boot.

Washington urged Congress to award Lafayette a command: "He is sensible—discreet in his manners—has made great proficiency in our Language, and from the disposition he discovered at the Battle of Brandy Wine, possesses a large share of bravery and Military ardor."

Congress eventually agreed.

In late 1777, there was a movement to replace Washington with General Horatio Gates. Lafayette wrote, "The people become attached to victorious generals, and the commander in chief had not been fortunate. . . . [I] was attached to [Washington] . . . and [I] did not waver. Despite the flatteries of the other party, [I] remained faithful."

He declared in a letter, "Our general is a man truly made for this revolution, which could not succeed without him."

The happiness of America is intimately connected with the happiness of all mankind.
—MARQUIS DE LAFAYETTE

No enemies to that great man can be found except among the enemies to his country; nor is it possible for any man of a noble spirit to refrain from loving the excellent qualities of his heart.
—MARQUIS DE LAFAYETTE, REFERRING TO GEORGE WASHINGTON

The movement failed.

By September 1778, Lafayette's dedication still had not wavered. He wrote to Washington, "As long as you fight I want to fight along with you." But in December, he was compelled to return to his native country. A war was brewing in Europe.

Washington wrote Lafayette, "I am persuaded, my dear marquis, that there is no need of fresh proofs to convince you either of my affection for you personally, or of the high opinion I entertain of your military talents and merits. . . . Adieu, my dear marquis; my best wishes will ever attend you."

Lafayette wrote Washington, "Farewell, my most beloved general; it is not without emotion, I bid you this last adieu, before so long a separation. Don't forget an absent friend, and believe me for ever and ever, with the highest respect and tenderest affection."

Lafayette served France against England. In 1780, at the end of his campaign, he returned to America.

Washington's "eyes filled with tears of joy" when he received the dispatch: Lafayette was on his way!

Lafayette brought great news: he had convinced the French king to send troops to aid the American cause!

Lafayette contributed to the country's victory. He and his troops trapped British general Lord Cornwallis and his men at Yorktown, Virginia, until the American and French armies arrived.

The Battle of Yorktown was the last major conflict of the war. Two years later, in 1783, the war would formally end.

Lafayette returned to France. He and Washington wrote each other—even more when Washington retired. And they exchanged gifts.

Lafayette returned to America in 1784 for a two-week visit at Mount Vernon, Washington's home.

Bidding Lafayette farewell, the heartsick Washington sensed he would never see his adopted son again. Washington was "of a short lived family, and might soon expect to be entombed."

Lafayette refused to accept Washington's prediction. "My whole soul revolts at the idea," he wrote. "To you I shall return, and, within the walls of Mount Vernon, we shall yet often speak of old times."

Now, Lafayette had his own war to fight.

At the beginning of the French Revolution, Lafayette ordered the Bastille—a hated prison and "fortress of despotism"—destroyed.

He sent Washington its key, with this note: "It is a tribute which I owe as a son to my adoptive father, as an aid de camp to my General, as a Missionary of Liberty to its Patriarch."

Washington treasured this tribute to liberty but worried about Lafayette's safety.

He was right.

France's revolution did not go well. Lafayette was forced to flee—or lose his head.

Captured at the Austrian border, Lafayette would spend five years in prison. With his hands politically tied, Washington could do nothing. (He did provide asylum for Lafayette's son, George Washington Lafayette.)

Released in 1797, Lafayette still couldn't visit his beloved general. Tensions were stirring between the United States and France. People feared that war would erupt. Washington advised him to stay away.

He did.

Too long.

On December 14, 1799, George Washington died.

Lafayette mourned the loss of his "friend and father."

He returned to his beloved America one last time in 1824—for just over a year, in anticipation of the nation's fiftieth-anniversary celebration of American independence.

He visited Washington's tomb at Mount Vernon. Alone in the underground chamber, Lafayette wept.

Adieu, mon général.

Adieu.

THE LIFE OF LAFAYETTE

I do most devoutly wish that we had not a single Foreigner among us, except the Marquis de la Fayette.

—GEORGE WASHINGTON

1757 September 6—Born in rural southern France.

1759 August 1—Lafayette's father, an officer in the French army, is killed during the Seven Years' War; his mother moves to Paris, and he is raised in the country by his grandmother.

1768 September—Moves to Paris at age eleven to join his mother; attends the College du Plessis.

1770 April 3—Lafayette's mother dies at age thirty-three.
April 11—Joins the King's Musketeers (influenced by his grandfather's military experiences).
April 24—Lafayette becomes one of the wealthiest aristocrats in Europe by inheriting his maternal grandfather's fortune.
September—Applies for appointment to the King's Musketeers' corps d'élite.

1771 April 9—Appointed to serve in the corps d'élite; enters the Military Academy at Versailles.

1774 April 11—Fourteen-year-old Adrienne Noailles becomes Lafayette's wife. He is now a brevet lieutenant in the prestigious Noailles Regiment.

1775 August 8—Meets the Duke of Gloucester, brother of King George III of Great Britain. After learning about the rebellious colonists in America, he is resolved to join them.
December 15—Adrienne gives birth to a daughter, Henriette.

1776 December 7—American commissioner Silas Deane contracts Lafayette to become a major general in the Continental army; Lafayette finances his own ship, *La Victoire*.

1777 April 20—Sets sail for America, sneaking out of France without permission.

June 13—Lands in South Carolina.

July 1—Adrienne gives birth to a second daughter, Anastasie.

July 27—Arrives in Philadelphia.

July 31—Congress appoints Lafayette an honorary major general in the American army; meets George Washington at City Tavern in Philadelphia.

September 11—Wounded at the Battle of Brandywine.

October 3—First daughter, Henriette, dies.

November—Rejoins Washington.

December—Congress gives Lafayette an official command as major general.

1779 January 11—Returns to France to fight in the country's war against England; requests aid for the American cause.

December 24—Adrienne gives birth to a boy, George Washington Lafayette.

1780 April 28—Returns to America, docking in Massachusetts; brings news for Washington: French troops are coming to help!

1781 August through September—Corners British general Lord Cornwallis at Yorktown, Virginia.

September 28–October 19—Washington joins Lafayette for final battle against Cornwallis; they are victorious.

December 23—Returns to France.

1783 May—Awarded France's highest military honor, the Cross of St. Louis, for his feats in the Revolutionary War.

September—Treaty of Paris is signed, making the United States' independence official. Adrienne gives birth to a daughter named Virginie—after the Commonwealth of Virginia where Washington lives.

1784 June—Leaves Paris to visit Washington at Mount Vernon; joins the French government upon his return, determined to bring liberty to his country.

1787 Harvard and the University of Pennsylvania award Lafayette with honorary doctorates in law. He also is given honorary American citizenship by Maryland, Massachusetts, and Virginia.

1789 July 11—Introduces his draft of the Declaration of the Rights of Man and the Citizen to the National Assembly in Paris (French Revolution begins on July 14); orders the destruction of the Bastille and sends its key to Washington.

1790 Princeton University awards Lafayette with an honorary doctorate in law.

1792 August 10—French monarchy is overthrown.

August 14—Lafayette flees when his execution is ordered.

August 19—Lafayette is captured at the Austrian border and imprisoned for five years.

1795 April—Fearing for her son's safety, Adrienne sends George Washington Lafayette to stay with George Washington at Mount Vernon.

October 15—Adrienne and their daughters move to Olmutz Prison to be with Lafayette.

1797 September 19—Lafayette, his wife, and their daughters are freed. President George Washington and the U.S. government help negotiate this.

1798 February—George Washington Lafayette returns to France from the United States, reuniting the family.

1799 French dictator Napoléon Bonaparte rises to power to Lafayette's dismay. They do not like each other. Lafayette spends the remainder of his life fighting for justice for the common man.

1807 December 24—Adrienne dies after a lingering illness, most likely originating from her stay at Olmutz.

1824 August 15—Arrives in America as "The Nation's Guest"; tours for a year, visiting all twenty-four states; hailed as a hero—and as an American—and stirs national pride. Many towns, cities, streets, and institutions are named in his honor.

1830 July—Takes command of the French National Guard; continues to argue for democracy.

1834 May 20—Dies at age seventy-six and is buried next to his wife. His body is covered with the American soil brought back from his trip to America.

THE LIFE OF GEORGE WASHINGTON

It should be the highest ambition of every American to extend his views beyond himself and to bear in mind that his conduct will not only affect himself, his country, and his immediate posterity; but that its influence may be co-extensive with the world, and stamp political happiness or misery on ages yet unborn.

—George Washington

1732 February 22—Born in Westmoreland County, Virginia. Washington's father, a remarried widower, has two sons and a daughter. George is the first of his parents' six children.

1735 Washington's family moves up the Potomac River to the Little Hunting Creek Plantation, later renamed Mount Vernon.

1738 The family moves again, to a plantation near Fredericksburg, Virginia. Washington spends much of his youth here.

1743 Washington's father dies. Washington inherits his family's plantation, Ferry Farm.

1748 Joins a surveying expedition, which leads to an appointment as a county surveyor.

1751 Accompanies his brother Lawrence to the British island colony of Barbados; sees military fortifications and socializes with soldiers; contracts smallpox.

1752 Lawrence dies. Mount Vernon is left to his young daughter.

1753 Takes Lawrence's position in the militia as a major; shows resilience on a nine-hundred-mile mission that earns him an international reputation by the next spring, at age twenty-two.

1754 Lieutenant Colonel George Washington is dispatched with 150 men to approach French troops and assert Virginia's demand for the land now claimed by France. Washington's men ambush French soldiers, killing ten and taking the rest prisoner. Washington retreats to a fort he calls "Necessity" but is forced to surrender when French soldiers surround the fort. Washington is humiliated, and the French and Indian War is ignited. Washington resigns his commission. Lawrence's daughter dies. Washington rents Mount Vernon from Lawrence's widow.

1755 Washington returns to fight as a volunteer. In battle, his commander is killed. Washington has two horses shot out from under him and four bullet holes in his coat, but he remains calm and leads the surviving men to safety. Because of his valor, Washington is given command of Virginia's entire military force.

1758 The British finally prevail and peace is restored. Washington is elected to the Virginia House of Burgesses, resigns his commission, and returns to Mount Vernon.

1759 Marries Martha Dandridge Custis, a young widow of one of the wealthiest men in Virginia; dedicates himself to working as a gentleman farmer; becomes stepfather to her two children.

1761 Lawrence's widow dies. Washington becomes the owner of Mount Vernon.

1774 August 5—Becomes one of seven Virginia delegates at the First Continental Congress.

1775 June 19—Commissioned by Congress to take command of the Continental army, which keeps him away from Mount Vernon for eight years.

1783 December 23—Appears before Congress in Annapolis, Maryland, and resigns his commission after the Treaty of Paris is signed with Great Britain; returns home with the intention of never serving in public life again.

1787 Ends his retirement and attends a convention to make changes to the Articles of Confederation; chosen to preside over the Constitutional Convention.

1788 The U.S. Constitution is ratified. Washington hopes to retire again.

1789 The first presidential election is held. Washington receives a vote from every elector. He remains the only U.S. president elected unanimously.

1789–1797 Serves two terms as president; refuses a third term and again retires to Mount Vernon.

1799 December 12—Falls ill after riding in a snow and sleet storm.
December 14—Dies at age sixty-seven with his wife at his side.

PLACES TO VISIT

NEW JERSEY
Monmouth Battlefield State Park
16 Business Route 33
Manalapan
state.nj.us/dep/parksandforests/parks/monbat.html

This park preserves the area where the Battle of Monmouth was waged. Roam the land where soldiers fought. See the visitors' center and a restored Revolutionary War–era farmhouse. Experience the fight during the yearly reenactment, held each June.

NEW YORK
Park Avenue Armory
643 Park Avenue
New York City
armoryonpark.org

In the Colonel's Reception Room, a portrait of Lafayette faces a portrait of Washington. The room is used for receptions by the National Guard, which Lafayette is credited with naming.

NORTH CAROLINA
Fayetteville
visitfayettevillenc.com

In 1783, Campbellton, North Carolina, was renamed in honor of Lafayette. Fayetteville was the first U.S. city named after the marquis and the only one he visited (in 1825). On Gillespie Street, you'll find a marker indicating where he stayed.

PENNSYLVANIA
Brandywine Battle Historic Site
1491 Baltimore Pike
Chadds Ford
ushistory.org/Brandywine

Site of the battle that led to the Americans' loss of Philadelphia and where Lafayette was wounded. Take one of three driving tours to retrace the troops' steps and visit sites of interest. Check the website for dates of reenactments and events.

City Tavern
138 South Second Street
Philadelphia
citytavern.com

City Tavern's mission is to provide diners with a culinary experience reminiscent of colonial days. The menu is authentic, and the décor is restored.

Independence National Historical Park
143 South Third Street
Philadelphia
nps.gov/inde

Visit the place where dreams of independence became real. This park spans more than fifty-five acres on twenty city blocks within Philadelphia, including the location of the First and Second Continental Congresses and where the Declaration of Independence, the Articles of Confederation, and the Constitution of the United States of America were debated and signed. Free guided tours are available. And, of course, see the most famous symbol of our freedom: the Liberty Bell.

Valley Forge National Historical Park
1400 North Outer Line Drive
King of Prussia
nps.gov/vafo/index.htm

Washington's ragged troops endured the brutal winter of 1777–1778 here. Visit the museum, which features a film and Revolutionary War artifacts. Outside, take a guided tour—or dial up a cell-phone tour! Check the website for seasonal and annual programs, many geared for kids.

VIRGINIA
Colonial National Historical Park (Yorktown Battlefield)
1000 Colonial Parkway
Yorktown
nps.gov/colo

See where Lafayette cornered British general Lord Cornwallis, which led to an American victory and the end of the Revolutionary War. Take one of two self-guided auto tours, and visit historic Yorktown while you're there. Check the website for events and children's activities.

Colonial Williamsburg
101 Visitor Center Drive
Williamsburg
history.org

Experience the eighteenth century in the world's largest living-history museum. In this reconstructed colonial capital (hundreds of homes, shops, and public buildings have been re-created on more than three hundred acres—most on their original locations), costumed historical interpreters bring the eighteenth century alive. You never know who you'll meet— perhaps even Lafayette!

George Washington's Mount Vernon Estate, Museum, and
   Gardens
3200 Mount Vernon Memorial Highway
Alexandria
mountvernon.org
   Lafayette visited Washington at his beloved homestead.
Years later, Lafayette returned to Mount Vernon and wept
in Washington's tomb. Today, you can enjoy an elaborate
museum and education center. Tour the grounds and pause
at Washington's current and former tombs. At the mansion,
relax on the back porch overlooking the Potomac River—just as
Washington and Lafayette did. Visit the website for special events.

FRANCE
Château Lafayette
Le Puy-en-Velay, France
chateau-lafayette.com
   Explore the mansion where Lafayette grew up, including
the *chambre natale* where he was born. Learn about his
ancestry, watch a film about his achievements, and stroll the
beautiful gardens where Lafayette first mused about glory.

Picpus Cemetery
35 Picpus Street
Paris
pariscemeteries.com (Les Cimetières de Paris; click on "Picpus")
   In a span of one month and four days during the summer
of 1794, this former neighborhood garden was transformed
into a mass grave to accommodate 1,306 guillotined men
and women during the French Revolution. Lafayette and his
family narrowly escaped the guillotine, but some of his wife's
family did not. When Picpus became a traditional cemetery,
a prerequisite to burial there was the loss of a relative on the
guillotine that cruel summer. Lafayette and his wife, Adrienne,
rest near the entrance to that mass grave, and a U.S. flag flies at
his side. This flag is replaced every Independence Day in a joint
French-American ceremony.

LAFAYETTE'S LEGACY IN AMERICA

   Lafayette helped secure the independence of the United
States. When he returned in 1824 as "The Nation's Guest," he
ignited a new pride in the country's history.
   Dozens of U.S. cities, towns, counties, and streets are
named after him. Lafayette College in Easton, Pennsylvania,
was chartered shortly after his final visit. There are monuments
and statues honoring Lafayette in several cities. In Washington,
D.C.—adjacent to the White House—lies Lafayette Square Park.

BIBLIOGRAPHY

All quotations used in the book can be found in the following
sources marked with an asterisk (*).

PAPERS (Primary Sources)
*Arthur H. and Mary Marden Dean Lafayette Collection,
   1520–1849. Carl A. Kroch Library, Division of Rare and
   Manuscript Collections, Cornell University Library.
   (Relevant selections from this collection were compiled by
   Stanley J. Idzerda. See next page.)

*George Washington Papers at the Library of Congress,
   1741–1799. Manuscript Division, Library of Congress.

*Letter from George Washington to Gouverneur Morris, July 24,
   1778. George Washington's Mount Vernon Estate, Museum,
   and Gardens Research Databases. The Papers of George
   Washington, Digital Edition, the University of Virginia Press.
   mountvernon.org/educational-resources/research/databases.

BOOKS
Alden, John R. *George Washington: A Biography*. Baton Rouge:
   Louisiana State University Press, 1984.

Bakeless, John. *Turncoats, Traitors, and Heroes*. Philadelphia:
   J. B. Lippincott, 1959.

Bernier, Olivier. *Lafayette: Hero of Two Worlds*. New York:
   E. P. Dutton, 1983.

Billias, George Athan, ed. *George Washington's Generals
   and Opponents: Their Exploits and Leadership*. New York:
   Da Capo Press, 1994.

Chase, P. D., F. E. Grizzard Jr., D. R. Hoth, E. G. Lengel, et al., eds.
   The Papers of George Washington. Revolutionary War Series.
   20 vols. Charlottesville: University Press of Virginia, 1985–2010.

Chinard, Gilbert, ed. and trans. *George Washington as the
   French Knew Him: A Collection of Texts*. Princeton, NJ:
   Princeton University Press, 1940.

Clary, David A. *Adopted Son: Washington, Lafayette, and the
   Friendship That Saved the Revolution*. New York: Bantam Dell,
   2007.

Ferling, John E. *The First of Men: A Life of George Washington*.
   Knoxville: University of Tennessee Press, 1988.

Fitzpatrick, John C., ed. *The Diaries of George Washington, 1748–1799*. Vol. 2, 1771–1785. Boston: Houghton Mifflin, 1925.

Flexner, James Thomas. *George Washington in the American Revolution, 1775–1783*. Boston: Little, Brown, 1968.

Flexner, James Thomas. *Washington: The Indispensable Man*. Boston: Little, Brown, 1974.

Freeman, Douglas Southall. *George Washington: A Biography*. New York: Charles Scribner's Sons, 1952.

Fritz, Jean. *Why Not, Lafayette?* Illustrated by Ronald Himler. New York: Penguin Putnam Books for Young Readers, 1999.

Gaines, James R. *For Liberty and Glory: Washington, Lafayette, and Their Revolutions*. New York: W. W. Norton, 2007.

*Gottschalk, Louis. *Lafayette in America*. Arveyres, France: L'Esprit de Lafayette Society, 1975. Combines portions of three previously published works by Gottschalk: *Lafayette Comes to America*, 1935; *Lafayette Joins the American Army*, 1937; and *Lafayette and the Close of the American Revolution*, 1942, with the final portion added in 1975.

*Gottschalk, Louis, ed. *The Letters of Lafayette to Washington, 1777–1799*. Philadelphia: American Philosophical Society, 1976.

*Idzerda, Stanley J., ed. *Lafayette in the Age of the American Revolution: Selected Letters and Papers, 1776–1790*. Ithaca, NY: Cornell University Press, 1977.

Jackson, Donald, and Dorothy Twohig, eds. *The Diaries of George Washington*. Charlottesville: University of Virginia Press, 1976.

Kinnaird, Clark. *George Washington: The Pictorial Biography*. New York: Hastings House, 1967.

*Lafayette, Marie. *Memoirs, Correspondence, and Manuscripts of General Lafayette*. Charleston, SC: BiblioBazaar, 2006.

Levasseur, Auguste. *Lafayette in America, in 1824 and 1825: Journal of a Voyage to the United States*. Translated by Alan R. Hoffman. Manchester, NH: Lafayette Press, 2006. Originally published in French in 1829.

Rudder, John B., and Diane Windham Shaw. *A Son and His Adoptive Father: The Marquis de Lafayette and George Washington*. Mount Vernon, VA: Mount Vernon Ladies' Association, 2006. (A companion to a traveling exhibition organized by the Mount Vernon Ladies' Association.)

Staib, Walter. *City Tavern Cookbook: 200 Years of Classic Recipes from America's First Gourmet Restaurant*. Philadelphia: Running Press, 1999.

Tallmadge, Benjamin. *Memoir of Colonel Benjamin Tallmadge*. New York: Thomas Holman, 1858.

Villanueva, Marcel. *The French Contribution to the Founding of the United States*. New York: Vantage Press, 1975.

ADDITIONAL SOURCES

City Tavern, Philadelphia, Pennsylvania.

David Library of the American Revolution, Washington Crossing, Pennsylvania.

*George Washington's Mount Vernon Estate, Museum, and Gardens, Virginia ("Washington's Legacy," mountvernon.org).

A Son and His Adoptive Father: The Marquis de Lafayette and George Washington. Exhibition sponsored by the New-York Historical Society, New York, New York, November 13, 2007–March 9, 2008.

FRENCH PHRASES (In Order of Appearance)

C'est le moment—this is the time
Mais non—but no
Magnifique—magnificent
Au contraire—on the contrary
Très bien—very good (literally translated: very well)
Maintenant—now
Enchanté—pleased to meet you (literally translated: enchanted)
Voilà—there you have it
Une situation grave—a serious situation
Bon—nice (literally translated: good)
S'il vous plaît—please (literally translated: if you please)
Quel honneur—what an honor
Zut alors—drat
Sacrebleu—a cry of distress or surprise
Mon Dieu—(oh) my God
Immédiatement—immediately
Allez—go
Adieu, mon général—good-bye, my general

CONGRESS SALUTES THE REVOLUTIONARY FRIENDSHIP

In the chamber of the U.S. House of Representatives, two portraits hang beside the Speaker's rostrum (a place for public speaking, where the Speaker of the House presides). They have been there since the opening of the current chamber in 1858. To the left of the rostrum is a painting of the Marquis de Lafayette. To the right hangs one of George Washington.

French artist Ary Scheffer painted *Gilbert du Motier, Marquis de Lafayette* in 1823 and presented it to the U.S. House of Representatives in 1824.

American artist John Vanderlyn was commissioned in 1834 to paint *George Washington* as a companion to Scheffer's *Lafayette*.